Crewe & Cheshire

Scenes From The 1980s

Terry Moors

Landmark Publishing

Published by

The Oaks, Moor Farm Road West, Ashbourne, DE6 1HD
Tel: (01335) 347349
Fax: (01335) 347303
email: landmark@clara.net

1st Edition

13 ISBN: 978-1-84306-405-3

Print: TJ International, Cornwall
Design by: Michelle Prost

Front Cover: Class 40 No 40001 approaches Nantwich station heading for Gresty Lane with a ballast train
on 7th June 1982 as two elderly pedestrians wait for the gates to be opened.

Back Cover Main: A view of the passageway between No 2 and No 1 platforms on 26th September 1984
and the place is a hive of activity as an AC electric glides into No 1 platform with an Anglo-Scottish express
and porters rush through with carts full of mail.

Back cover Bottom Left: One of the four decorative cast iron Eagles recovered from the 'Eagle Bridge',
which was situated on Crewe Works, now takes a prominent place at the entrance to the appropriately
named 'Eagle Bridge Health and Wellbeing Centre' in Dunwoody Way. The centre is built on part of the
Works known as the Stone Yard.

Page 3: On 21st August 1988 the first of many steam-hauled passenger excursions from Crewe to the
North Wales coast commenced with Ex LMS 4-6-2 No 6201 'Princess Elizabeth', seen here racing through
Tarporley on the return working of that inaugural run.

Crewe & Cheshire Railways
Scenes From The 1980s

Terry Moors

Landmark Publishing

CONTENTS

GLOSSARY

ECS	Empty Coaching/Carriage Stock
Diagram	A schedule designed to obtain the most efficient working arrangement for train crews, locomotives and rolling stock.
Head shunt	A length of track, which allows shunting movements to be made into a cluster of sidings without fouling the running lines to which it is connected.
LMS	London Midland & Scottish Railway
MGR	Merry-go-Round. A system of operating continuously moving permanently coupled trains between collieries and electricity generating power stations.
NSR	North Staffordshire Railway Company
TOPS	British Railways' computer-based Total Operations Processing System of freight wagon information, introduced in 1973. It details every event concerning freight traffic (and locomotives and other items of stock) and transmits this information over the whole of British Rail.
ZUV	Three-letter TOPS code (as an example) for a 'Shark' ballast plough. (codes for other types of freight wagons appear at various points in the text)
BREL	British Rail Engineering limited
CLC	Cheshire Lines committee
GJR	Grand Junction Railway
LMWR	London & North Western Railway, also the current commercial of Peter Waterman

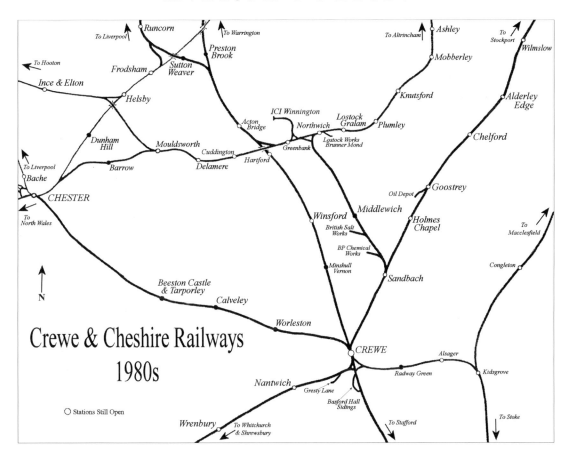

Crewe & Cheshire Railways 1980s

O Stations Still Open

I can say without hesitation that my interest in railways has not diminished even a little over the last 55 years. I still remember, as a five-year old on a cold winter's evening, hearing distant 'mysterious' and almost haunting sounds. I later discovered they were the syncopated exhaust beats of steam locomotives. It was 1950 and the place was my home village of Chell, Stoke-on-Trent. The locomotives were industrial tank engines working the mineral line from Pinnox Sidings, Tunstall to Chatterley Whitfield Colliery near to Fegg Hayes. This mineral line was quite steeply graded in places, and I used to watch them negotiate at speed an unmanned and un-gated crossing over Little Chell Lane before passing into a 404-yard tunnel beneath High Lane, Chell known locally as "The Suff", after which the train ran approximately one mile to the colliery.

By 1953 the family had moved to Tunstall and here my railway horizons broadened to spotting trains on the nearby Loop Line and observing express passenger engines working through Longport. A year or so later we moved a mile north to Goldenhill, where only a short distance from home

I 'found' Kidsgrove station from where I eventually took the opportunity to make Saturday trips to Crewe station by train.

I was ten years old when I made my first 'solo' trip to Crewe, just prior to local steam-hauled services being replaced by new diesel multiple units (DMUs). By 1957 the DMUs had taken over the Derby-Crewe services and I have to admit they did provide a much better view for an eager train-spotter especially if you could get a seat behind the driver. Regular weekend visits to Crewe followed, supplemented by weekday trips during the summer holidays, which only strengthened my interest in railways and from then on I was 'hooked'.

During this time it became fairly obvious that things were changing on the railway and by 1960 the old station frontage on Nantwich Road was demolished and replaced with a 'modern' entrance canopy, foyer, ticketing counters and barriers. Motive power was also changing with certain steam-worked diagrams being turned over to diesel traction and

North Shed, the bastion of top link passenger steam engines, began to accommodate and service Type 4 diesel locos. Also in 1960 the Crewe to Manchester line was electrified and bright 'Electric Blue' AL1 electric locomotives could be seen wafting around the station accompanied by the distinctive sound of their traction motor blowers.

The next few years witnessed great changes on the railway network that culminated with a steam-hauled passenger train, the "Fifteen Guinea Special" on 11th August 1968, bringing an end to steam operation on British Railways. This was a life-changing event for some railway workers; particularly loco firemen who sadly found themselves out of a job. The railway continued however, unmoved by the loss of steam, with diesel and electric traction seamlessly taking its place. The next twelve years seemed to pass with little obvious change except that the once familiar express passenger trains became part of a network of 'Inter City' services and almost all locomotives and coaching stock took on the dreary 'BR' blue and blue/grey livery.

Throughout the 20-year period between 1960 and 1980 I regret to say that I undertook very little railway photography and of this only a few negatives survived a house move in the 1970s. But from 1980 onwards, being aware then that there were plans afoot to change the railway scene, especially those proposed for Crewe Station, I decided that I should try to re-store the balance. So, it was the summer of 1980 that I rekindled my railway spotting days, travelling by train once again from Kidsgrove to Crewe Station and took up my favourite place at the south end of No 4 Platform-but this time it was to take photographs not loco numbers.

During the years that followed I photographed the changing railway scene, concentrating initially on my home ground in North Staffordshire and then Cheshire, in particular Crewe Station and Crewe Locomotive Works, interspersed with a number of excursions into Derbyshire.

From this photographic record came my first book 'North Staffordshire Railways Scenes from the 1980s', which concentrated on the lines around Stoke-on-Trent and Newcastle under Lyme. So it probably comes as no surprise that this second volume covers Crewe and the lines into Cheshire. It follows the same format as the North Staffordshire book and comprises perhaps a wider area although two of the chapters, Crewe Station and Crewe Locomotive Works, are justifiably given extended coverage since they have both experienced significant loss of infrastructure.

Again this book is about pictures, which I hope will bring back memories of happier times to those who were spotting trains during that decade and provide a pictorial legacy to the latest generation of railway enthusiasts. Hopefully it will also be a source of interesting images for the non-railway reader to illustrate railway travel as it was 25 years ago.

In compiling this book I have sought the help of a number of friends and acquaintances and indeed people I have never met before. They have all provided that help without hesitation, be it photographs, books and publications, maps or just plain but nevertheless important items of information. My sincere thanks therefore go to Peter Rawlins, Martin Steventon and Peter Thorley for allowing me to use some of their photographs. David Thornton for his assistance with locomotive identification, Spencer Jackson for information regarding the modernisation of Crewe Station and Keith Swift for helping me to identify certain locations in Crewe Works. Lastly, my thanks to Landmark Publishing for allowing me the freedom to select all of the pictures. I have taken care in ensuring dates, times and location details are accurate but like most publications errors and omissions do appear and I take full responsibility for these. If any errors or omissions do surface I would be grateful for the reader to advise me accordingly.

Terry Moors
Goldenhill

BIBLIOGRAPHY

Whilst compiling Crewe & Cheshire Railways Scenes From The 1980s I referred to various sources including magazines and periodicals and the following publications, some of which are now out of print.

Baker, Allan C *Crewe Remembered* (Irwell Press)

Baker, Allan C & Morrison, Gavin *Crewe Sheds* (Ian Allan)

Baker, S.K. *Rail Atlas Great Britain & Ireland 11th Edition* (Oxford Publishing Co)

Dyckhoff, Nigel *Portrait of The Cheshire Lines Committee* (Ian Allan)

Marsden, Colin J *Rolling Stock Recognition-Departmental Stock* (Ian Allan)

Marsden, Colin J *Rolling Stock Recognition-BR and Private Owner Wagons* (Ian Allan)

Oppitz, Leslie *Cheshire Railways Remembered* (Countryside Books)

Wilkinson, Allan *British Railway Pictorial: Crewe North* (Ian Allan)

CHAPTER 1: CREWE STATION

Without doubt Crewe Railway Station is one of the most historic stations in the world. The story began at 8.45am on 4th July 1837 when the Grand Junction Railway (GJR) opened its line between Warrington and Birmingham and the very first passenger train stopped at Crewe. The station was named after the Earl of Crewe whose mansion, Crewe Hall, stood nearby. The area at the time was known as Monks Coppenhall but as the GJR had purchased land from the Earl's estate the company decided that Crewe was a good name for its station. Within three years Crewe had become an operating centre for the GJR when they transferred locomotive and carriage building from Edge Hill. When the GJR became part of the London & North Western Railway (LNWR) Crewe was by then a growing railway town and in 1861 the population numbered 18,000. The LNWR was a great benefactor to Crewe when at the turn of the century most of the town's 40,000 inhabitants worked for the railway and its Locomotive Works. Most of that legacy was still in place during the 1980s when Crewe station remained a very busy junction, almost unaltered except for a refurbishment to the station frontage and road bridge in 1960. From 2nd June until 21st July 1985 the station was closed to all train services, with the exception of two DMU shuttle services, whilst the station underwent a complete transformation. This chapter provides views of the station during a decade that brought about some of the greatest changes since it was built.

This is a view of the station entrance on 13th February 1983 when, as a prelude to the main closure in 1985, the concourse and ticket counters were about to be renovated. It shows the 1960s style frontage and when viewed from the same spot today it still looks very similar in appearance except the canopy angle is now extended outwards and the island, once used for taxis and buses, has been removed. *(Peter Thorley)*

On 7th December 1981 Advanced Passenger Train (APT) No 370002 glides into the station's single Up through road (ruling speed 15mph) whilst working the APT's first public passenger run from Glasgow to London Euston. Following years of development problems it was hoped that this scheduled run would mark a successful start to fast APT operations on the West Coast Main line. Unfortunately, the train experienced technical problems just north of Watford and the APT never went into regular passenger service.

The first AC electric to be introduced in regular service with British Railways was E3001 (81001). Built by AEI (BTH)/BRCW in November 1959 the locomotive is seen here standing at platform 6b on 7th December 1981 with parcels and newspaper vans ready to be offloaded. The locomotive, which was given the name *'Envoy'* in 1965 but never used, was badly damaged by fire at Carstairs whilst working a Motorail train on 26th August 1983. It was subsequently scrapped at BREL Crewe in 1986.

When this picture was taken on 9th December 1981 class 33s had started to replace class 25s on the Crewe to South Wales services. Although the 33s were always 'Southern' engines, some creative diagramming by the Southern Region meant they were able to work these locomotives as far north as Crewe. Standing at platform 4b class 33/1 No 33031 is being coupled to its train, the 1020hrs Crewe-Cardiff.

Activity at Crewe Sorting Sidings as class 86 No 86001 arrives with a train of privately owned PJA/PJB double-deck 'Cartic 4' sets, operated by Tolemans Delivery Services. These wagons were permanently coupled in 4-car sets having articulated bogies joining each vehicle. Seven sets of four-car Cartics formed the average train with a capacity of approximately 170 cars. The Carriage sidings can be seen in the background whilst the large buildings in the background form part of the steel foundry operated by Midland Rollermakers Ltd. 86001 is now in preservation with the AC Locomotive Group.

This is a view of Crewe Sorting Sidings North signal box looking north in the direction of the station. This particular box, built by BR (LMR), opened on 3rd June 1962, replacing the original LNWR signal cabin that opened in October 1901. The current box, still in use, is a substantial affair with a 95-lever Crewe electric IFS panel controlling a web of lines into Basford Hall. In the left distance is the Transhipment Sheds with No 1 Up Arrival line in the left foreground. Swinging to the right of the box is the Down Engine line joining the Up Slow Goods line.

My good friend, the late Malcolm Kelly, was a real fan of class 40s and he took this photograph at North Sorting Sidings in May 1986. The line-up comprises 97407 (40012), complete with the white buffers, wind screen and wheels, 97408 (40118) and class 25/2 No 25212, their fate unknown. *(Malcolm Kelly)*

July 1984 and class 40 No 40104 is captured roaring away from the station on the Up through road with an engineers' spoil train towards South Junction. *(Peter Rawlins)*

Steam heat class 25 No 25027 ambles into No 4 platform with Inspection Saloon DBM999504 on 1st September 1982 following a trip over the North Stafford branch from Kidsgrove. There were three of these Inspection Saloons, built by BR on short wheelbase Mk1 vehicles and they had observation saloons at each end.

This picture of class 25 No 25221, one of the last of its class with an operating headcode box, shows the complex track layout at the south end of the station. All this was to change in the summer of 1985 when re-modelling work would reduce the total number of points and crossings from 285 to 110. 27th August 1983. *(Peter Rawlins)*

On 1st September 1982 class 08 No 08913 draws a rake of Mk 1 stock out of platform 4b following its earlier arrival from south Wales. The train engine would be detached in the bay platform ready to run forward whilst the 08 returns the coaches back into the platform to await the locomotive. This was one of many interesting train movements that were daily occurrences around the station at that time.

Crewe station had no fast through lines until the re-modelling was completed in July 1985. This picture shows No4 Carriage Siding (and engine holding road), which ran between platforms 4 and 5 for half the station's length. On 26th August 1983 an unusual visitor occupied the siding, class 120 3-car DMU in Trans Cly delivery still showing 'Glasgow Central' on the destination blind. *(Peter Thorley)*

Four years later, on 21st February 1987, a member of the former 'Glasgow Blue Train' class 303 No 303050 made an appearance at No 1 platform (originally No 6 platform) whilst working a Altrincham-Crewe service. The 303s were relocated to the Manchester area to operate the Hadfield service later that year following the route's conversion to 25Kv supply and the displacement of the old class 506 EMUs. *(Peter Thorley)*

In March 1981 class 86 No 86228 *'Vulcan Heritage'* stands at No 4 platform with a Glasgow-Euston train as the driver and guard exchange good-natured banter with two young enthusiasts, no doubt taking advantage of the time required to unload mail and parcels.

The same locomotive but with three different enthusiasts this time taking a 'brass rubbing' of the loco's nameplate. This was the sort of interest shown by young people in those days and some of this was down to the variety of motive power that worked the railway during the 1980s.

The famous footbridge that during the age of steam beckoned many a young train spotter to 'trespass' (including myself) into North Shed. Actually I can't recall anyone making it to the far side before a voice bellowed, "come down off there!" In July 1984, the steam shed had long since gone and the footbridge disused as class 40 No 40129 passes the station on No 1 through road with an unidentified class 47 on their way to the diesel depot. The tracks in the foreground are the Up and Down Chester Independent Lines. *(Peter Rawlins)*

June 1981 and Platform 4b is busy with the train engine, steam heat class 25 No 25042, about to buffer-up to an afternoon Crewe-Cardiff working, with a little encouragement from a young enthusiast beckoning from the coach door.

Darlington-built English Electric Class 40 No 40106 first gained the public gaze in 1979 when it was to become BR's last green-liveried main line locomotive. However, public interest was such that during its overhaul at Crewe that same year it was returned to service in green. Seen here at No 3 platform on 4th December 1984, it was waiting to depart with the first leg of a Vale of Rheidol Anniversary Special. After final withdrawal it passed into preservation at the Great Central Railway where it was named '*Atlantic Conveyor*' to commemorate a Falklands War loss.

Toton-based class 56 No 56042 makes a smoky departure from No 4 platform on 5th March 1983. Nothing extraordinary in that except the locomotive is riding on experimental bogies designed for class 58 locomotives.

On 4th December 1982 a watery sun peers through the morning mist as class 33 No 33013 stands in platform 4b waiting to depart with the 1020hrs Crewe-Cardiff. In the background a lone class 86 stands in Bank Engine siding.

Class 86/1 No 86103 *'Andre Chapelon'* waits for its scheduled departure from Crewe at 1008hrs whilst working the 0620hrs Glasgow-London Euston on 4th December 1983. This was one of three class 86/0 locomotives that were rebuilt with class 87 bogies and traction motors.

On 5th March 1983 two eager 'spotters' were coping with a sudden burst of activity with a train standing on the Up through line and 87021 *'Robert The Bruce'* drifting into No 5 Platform with an unidentified charter train. This locomotive was built in April 1974 and following withdrawal in 2005 it was sold for export to Bulgarian Railways.

The ramp at the south end of No 5 Platform was a good spot to view and photograph trains. Although having personally been cautioned by the BT Police for standing there I wouldn't recommend it. In this view 85022 waits for signals to depart with a rake of empty Mk 1 stock. This loco was built at BR Doncaster in March 1963 and interestingly it was allocated the name *'Emperor'* which was never applied. It was eventually scrapped in 1992 at MC Metals Glasgow.

Strolling in at line speed (15mph) on the Up through line, 47355 makes light work of failed AC electric 87028 *'Lord President'* and its unidentified train. I speculate that the 87 had failed since there was no P-Way engineering work in the area on that day, 5th March 1983.

On the same day 'double stamps' in the form of English Electric type 4s, 40086 and 40084 wait at No 4 Platform with 'The Silver Jubilee' railtour to commemorate 25 years service of the class 40s. Note that at this time the platform ended with the canopy. When the station was remodelled in 1985 the platform was extended 200 feet to accommodate longer trains. Also, prior to 1985, No 4 Platform was not bi-directional so it was unusual to see passengers boarding a southbound train here.

Previous to 1985 No 3 Platform was the station's only designated bi-directional platform and all other lines passed through the station as Up or Down lines only. On 4th December 1982 class 33 No 33013 faces south on No 3 Platform waiting to depart with a train of empty coaching stock.

On 28th September 1983 newly built class 56 No 56125 heads back to Crewe Works on the Down through line No2, as it returns from a load test to Shrewsbury with the Works test train.

On 16th June 1983 class 20s 20035 and 20070 leave North Stafford Junction and on to the Down through line No2 to pass through the station with an afternoon Oakamoor-St Helens sand train.

Later in the year, on 28th September 1983, class 40 No 40022 heads a similar sand train on the Down through road No2. To the left of the train is No2 Platform stacked with the piles of mailbags and parcels, which were a common sight at that time.

On 30th March 1983, in the space of two hours, I managed to photograph 31 individual locomotives, comprising 10 different classes, working a variety of passenger and freight trains. One example, not all that common at Crewe, was class 45 No 45141 that appeared light engine from the north and is seen here on the Up through line.

The south end of No4 Platform was well populated with enthusiasts on 28th December 1983 as 86243 arrives with an Anglo-Scottish train during the 'festive' week. The view from this particular spot is now quite different, since the platform was extended forwards 200 feet during the remodelling in 1985.

This photograph taken on 14th March 1984 shows the old track layout between platforms 4 and 5 as AC electrics 86221 and 86030 trundle past the station on the Up through line on their way to be stabled in Bank Engine Siding.

On the same day Class 81 No 81017 adds to the congestion on No 5 Platform as it arrives with an afternoon parcels train. One of the early AL1 locos it was built in April 1961 by AEI (BTH). It was withdrawn in the late 1980s and scrapped at Coopers, Sheffield, in 1991.

One of the finer sensations in life is the start of a train journey, and here rolling into No1 Platform on 10th March 1984, past the diminutive Station 'A' box, is 86317 with my train for that particular day, 'The Conway Crusader' railtour. The 86 stayed on as far as Manchester Piccadilly where it was replaced by class 40 No 40029 for onward haulage to Chester.

Another view of No 5 Platform as 86241 draws into the station with the 1515hrs Manchester Piccadilly-London Euston on 14th march 1984. For a long time the buildings on the right were derelict and although this was a principal platform there were no passenger facilities to be had.

I found the bay platforms always needed to be checked out since from time to time they would accommodate various items of interest. The 'North Stafford' platform, 5b was reserved almost exclusively for the Crewe-Derby trains, at this time mostly class 120 DMUs. Seen here on 14th March 1984 is a 3-car set which will form the 1620 Crewe-Lincoln. Standing in platform 6b are two GUVs coupled to a Mk1 First Open, which seemed to have been pressed into parcels traffic.

I arrived back into Crewe after a splendid day out as a passenger on 'The Conway Crusader' railtour that ended with class 50 haulage, taking in Llandudno and Blaenau Ffestiniog and then terminating, for me at least, at Crewe and I got this final picture of 50018 as it was about to depart No 5 Platform. 10th March 1984.

This picture, taken on 14th March 1984, shows the 'parcels' bays, 1b and 2b and middle 'bay siding'. Under the marvellous overall roof one of Crewe's class 08 shunters 08737, with its engine rumbling away, stands at Platform 2b a waiting its next duty.

Standing in the same spot on 9th February 2008 demolition on a huge scale had taken place. Rail House looks out on to this sad scene as contractors had already started backfilling. This area is now completely fenced off and No 1 platform is isolated and out of use.

In happier times, platform 2b accommodates one of Crewe's ZRV stores vans, XDE283799, which were used solely for transporting stationary. The building behind the van was once used as the Driver's signing-on rooms and later became part of the parcels admin offices. On the side of the van is written; *'To work between Crewe station-Crewe stationary stores only'*.

Bay Platform 4a was for a number of years used for Liverpool trains and seen here on 14th March 1984 is class 303 EMU 303067 having just arrived from Liverpool. The platform canopy may seem quite modern but it was actually built in 1955 as part of an early modernisation plan that ran through to 1960 when the electrification programme required major works to raise Nantwich Road Bridge.

Bay Platforms' 1a and 2a were originally known as the 'Chester Bays' and until 1985 a variety of services departed from these platforms, including a number of Crewe-Chester trains, which normally departed from Platform 3a. However on 14th March 1984 class 303 No 33078 utilised Platform 2a for the 1635hrs all-stations stopping service to Liverpool Lime Street.

When this picture was taken on 26th June 1985 the remodelling work was well underway and all track had been removed. An air of dereliction was already beginning to form as Platforms 2a and 3a, which were never again going to play host to summer holidaymakers waiting patiently for trains to take them to the seaside.

On 28th December 1983, shunter 08913 has just arrived at Platform 1b ready to bring out a number of parcels vans situated at the far end. Although the Christmas rush was over there was an extraordinary amount of mail and parcels arriving on that day.

Photographed from a similar spot eighteen months later, on 26th June 1985, the track had been removed and the bay was being used as a dump for used ballast and old fixtures and fittings.

The next few photographs illustrate the station on 26th September 1984 as 'Phase 1' work is carried out to provide Up and Down Fast Through Lines (80mph) and a complete refurbishment of No 5 Platform. This picture shows 47334 with a ballast train picking its way over newly laid track. In the middle foreground the incomplete Down Fast line stops short of an overhead support that would be removed at a later stage in the work.

As the work proceeded all southbound trains used No 4 Platform, including unidentified Motorail train, which is seen here passing through the station headed by class 81 No 81007 and a young enthusiast puts a parcels trolley to good use. The cars on board certainly date the scene!

Compare this picture with the one on page 22 and you can see how the new track layout is being formed. The new Up and Down Fast lines are roughly laid in place, ready for alignment and ballasting.

In this view, looking north from No 4 Platform, new track panels have been laid and in the left foreground a turnout that once connected with the old Up Through line is now isolated and the connection lifted.

Another view of Phase 1 track remodelling from No 4 Platform, looking south, where newly ballasted track (centre) has replaced the old No 4 Carriage Siding/Engine Release Road to form a new Down Fast Through line. In the background are wagons being used to bring in materials and removing spoil in connection with the renovation of No 5 Platform.

Looking north from the south end of No 4 Platform, track work progresses as class 86 No 86235 glides into the station, amidst all the hubbub of the engineering operations, for a scheduled stop whilst working a Glasgow-London Euston train.

On 25th April 1984 class 40 No 40057 'whistles' into platform 2a to provide motive power for an additional Holyhead service during a busy summer weekend. The photographer reminded me that these summer extras to Holyhead and the North Wales coast invariably produced a '40' off the Diesel Depot, in particular the 1727 Crewe-Holyhead. *(Martin Steventon)*

When this photograph was taken from the same spot on the 26th June 1985 all had changed and it shows the extent of that rationalisation as the remodelling of the station necessitated the removal of all track into bay platforms 2a and 3a, together with the approach lines. In the distance can be seen Crewe North Junction signal box and on the extreme left, where North Shed once stood, building work is underway on the new Signal Control Centre which would replace Crewe North, Crewe South and Station 'A' signal boxes.

By the end of June 1985 the remodelling work was well established and this view of No 5 Platform from the north steps shows the new track work was in place but at this stage devoid of overhead line equipment, which was due to be installed later in the programme of work. The once redundant buildings to the left were also given a new lease of life as they were being refurbished to provide waiting rooms, toilets, bookstall and a 'Travellers Fare' cafeteria. The new signage seems to acknowledge this already!

Another view of the north end of the station where new track alignments are almost complete but not yet connected to the main line. On the right, engineers' wagons stand at the new Bay Platform 9, (formerly Platform 4a) which has been extended by 110 feet to accommodate longer trains or multiple units. This platform became exclusive to Chester line trains since the remodelling work removed its direct connection to the main line.

Back to the 5th March 1983 and Class 86 No 86238 draws into No 4 Platform with a failed 86328 and its late-running London Euston-Manchester Piccadilly train consisting of new Mk 3 stock. The failed 86 was taken off here and transferred to the electric depot.

The same view on 26th June 1985 reveals not a foot of track remains as contractors' vehicles take to the trackbed to install new concrete foundations for overhead line supports. Prior to the track being lifted all the overhead lines were removed, as were other items of redundant electrical equipment.

On 26th November 1984 AC electrics 86327 and 86312 are about to pass behind Station 'A' signal box on the Down Through Line No1 on their way to the electric depot. All of this area has now been demolished and cleared.

This is a view of the Diesel Depot from No 1 Platform on 26th June 1985 as class 47 No 47470 'University of Edinburgh' heads towards the fuelling point over a temporary 'road' crossing. The holding sidings have taken on a role as a parking area for engineering vehicles and a stock ground for track panels.

During Phase 1 of the remodelling work, No 2 Platform became quite busy with northbound trains. On 26th September 1984 this view shows passengers beginning to gather for the next train and at the far end piles of mailbags and parcels fill the platform. Also, Station 'B' signal box was located in a space just behind the buffer stop. It was removed in 1940 when the new North Junction Signal Box was commissioned.

Twenty-three years on and the overall roof has gone, replaced by a modern cantilever type canopy. There are no mail trains now to create that wonderful 'busy' look to the platform. The trains however are very smart and capable as the Virgin Voyager units demonstrate, seen here having arrived on time with an afternoon Holyhead service on 11th July 2008.

During the station's closure all Inter City services were routed via the 'Independent Lines' but for passengers travelling to Crewe a DMU shuttle service operated from both Stafford and Chester. Seen here on 8th June 1985 a class 108/2 DMU ambles along the Independent Line with a positioning turn into the station. *(Peter Thorley)*

The only operational platform whilst the station underwent the remodelling was No 1 platform and this was restricted to the two DMU shuttle services. On 26th June 1985 a class 117/101 set stands at the north end of the platform ready to depart for Chester. No doubt the remaining passengers are waiting for the shuttle to Stafford – not that they had much choice!

On Monday 22nd July 1985 the big day arrived and Ms Gwynneth Dunwoody MP officially reopened the station to traffic. Later in the day as services were getting back to normal class 87 No 87032 glides into No 4 platform with the *'The Wessex Scot'* the 0900hrs Poole to Carstairs – at which point the train divides for Glasgow & Edinburgh. Without doubt the station had taken on a new and fresh appearance, No 5 platform in particular with its new passenger facilities, refurbished canopies, modern lighting and signage.

Reopening day again and class 86 No 86232 *'Harold Macmillan'* stands at No 5 platform with the 1325hrs Liverpool Lime Street to Plymouth.

Facing south from No 4 platform (formerly 5b) a summer shower highlights the new ballast in this view of a DMU standing at No 2 platform. During the remodelling this platform was extended by 375ft and at the same time it extended No 1 platform by an equal length enabling it to accommodate longer trains. 22nd July 1985.

On 24th May 1987 SPENO rail-grinding machine makes a visit to Crewe and is seen here doing a spot of 'fettling' on the Down Fast Through line. *(Peter Thorley)*

Birmingham-Liverpool services have produced a variety of motive power over the years and 16th July 1989 was no exception when class 31 No 31406 strides out of the station, past Crewe North Junction and the Heritage Centre, with an afternoon working to Liverpool. *(Peter Thorley)*

On 10th October 1985 class 58 power takes to the new Down Fast line as 58032 storms northwards with an MGR train. These new fast lines (up to 80mph) allowed more freight workings the opportunity of a direct route through the station.

Almost a year after the remodelling work a shabby looking class 25 No 25325 is not compelled to take the 'tradesman's' route around the station any more and is seen here rattling along the Down Fast line with an engineers' spoil train on 4th March 1986.

On 15th February 1987, in complete contrast to the above, the Venice Simplon Orient Express Pullmans wait on the Down Fast line whilst a change of locomotives is carried out. In absolutely immaculate condition Class 47 No 47638 takes charge as it prepares to haul the celebrated train on the next leg of a London Euston to Sale charter. Most of the passengers were in period costume and the lady seen at the first window has obviously buried herself in the part as she offers a 'Royal' wave to us 'riff raff' on the platform.

The little boy standing on No 4 platform is dwarfed by the two class 37s, No's 37680 and 37308 that were providing super-power for the 1245 Holyhead to London Euston on 9th July 1988. A footnote in the summer timetable reads: *"Timekeeping is subject to punctual arrival of the boat from Ireland"* With these two on the front I don't think timekeeping would have been a problem!

Crewe-Derby services during the 1980s produced some interesting haulage when failures occurred with the older DMU sets and even the sprinters from time to time. The early 1990s were no exception as seen here on 9th August 1990, when class 20s No's 20087 and 20058 and Mk2 stock leave platform 3 with an afternoon Crewe-Derby service. *(Peter Thorley)*

Class 90 No 90015 heads a rake of Railfreight Distribution ferry wagons north on the down fast through line on 18th February 1989. At the time class 90s were extremely rare on freight duties.

Coming off the Chester line on 18th February 1989, newly out-shopped from the works, class 91 No 91009 acquires the number 2 through road and heads south on a light trial run, possibly to Stafford and return.

As the end of 1990 draws near the sight of a Driving Van Trailer (DVT) at the head of an Inter City train (mainly southbound) was becoming quite common. On 3rd November 1990 DVT No 82103 draws away from No 5 platform with a not-so-common rake of Mk 3 Pullman cars working an afternoon Manchester to London Euston service and propelled by a class 86 AC electric.

Newly out shopped from Crewe Works class 86/4 No 86424 stands in the 'Salop' bay (platform 8) following a light trial run from the Works. This loco was built at Doncaster in May 1965 as E3111, then TOPS No 86024 and later renumbered 86324. As 86424 it is seen here equipped for multiple operation and in two-tone Railfreight grey but absent any sector logos. The loco is currently stored at LNWR Crewe as a Network Rail reserve locomotive.

During a guards dispute in Manchester some unusual stock movements took place. After coming off the Manchester line, class 31 No 31107 in 'Dutch Livery' trundles past the station on the up through road on 3rd November 1990 with Mk3 DVTs No's 82127 and 82146, destination unknown.

Class 90 No 90009 stands in Horse Landing Siding on 10th June 1989 waiting its next turn of duty. Behind the screen is the old No1 platform which by that time was disused. The line and platform in the right foreground is the Horse Dock, which was used during the 1980s to stable parcels vans and occasionally locomotives.

A view from the Nantwich Road bridge on 10th November 1990 with the overall roof still in place over the old No1 platform and the new platform12. The line running through the platform was in use at that time for locomotives proceeding to and from the Diesel Depot only. The lines on the right are Horse Landing Siding and Horse Dock respectively.

A picture taken from the same spot on 9th February 2008, following complete removal of the overall roof reveals the distinctive LNWR buildings, which were the offices of the Area Manager. The covered structure in the foreground is a pedestrian covered walkway that allows passengers, from platform 12, direct access to rail-replacement buses. The three tracks remain in place but now end at stop blocks just short of the walkway.

2: CREWE – SANDBACH – GOOSTREY

One of the early railways to make a connection with the Grand Junction Railway (GJR) at Crewe was the Manchester & Birmingham Railway (M&BR) which had ambitions to run a line from Manchester all the way to London. The main problem was the GJR, which had already established their Birmingham to Warrington line-and they had also built Crewe station. The GJR were not therefore overly sympathetic and resisted any attempt by the M&BR to operate beyond Crewe. But in 1842 the M&BR finally opened their line from Manchester London Road to Crewe, however trains ran only as far as Sandbach whilst the GJR decided if they would allow the M&BR into a designated platform at Crewe station. These inter-company disagree-ments were to disappear when, in 1846, both companies were incorporated into the London & North Western Railway Company (LNWR). The railway then oper-ated uneventfully for over a century until 1959 when the line became one of the first in the country to be electrified as part of the evolving 25Kv overhead sys-tem. The village of Goostrey was also made famous as the home of the World's largest Radio Telescopes at Jo-drell Bank. In the 1980s it was an interesting place to visit at weekends as numerous trains were diverted be-cause of engineering possessions on the North Stafford line through Stoke or on the West Coast Mainline. This chapter illustrates some of these workings along part of the line between Crewe and Chelford.

On 16th July 1989 class 31 No 31468, with a single parcels van, waits for signals at Crewe North Junction as a Manchester Piccadilly-Euston train proceeds off the Manchester line to join the West Coast Mainline seen running across the bottom of the picture. The open area to the left of the trains was once occupied by the LNWR's Grease Works, which recycled (for over 100 years!) used grease and oil recovered from the locomo-tive works. *(Peter Thorley)*

The first station after Crewe was Sandbach and seen here on 2nd October 1983 is class 310 EMU No 310060 arriving with the 1401 Birmingham New Street – Manchester Piccadilly. Interestingly the trackbed of the old North Stafford Railway line from Kidsgrove, via Wheelock, is still discernable as it curves in from the left beneath the lattice bridge to Foden's lorry works.

A view of Sandbach station on 2nd October 1983 as class 47 No 47530 storms through with the diverted 1150 Euston-Manchester Piccadilly. Just visible in the background, above the station buildings, is part of the extensive Foden Lorry Company's works.

Facing east at Sandbach as class 47 No 47350 races through with the diverted 1425 Manchester Piccadilly-Birmingham on 2nd October 1983. The tracks to the left of the island platform formed sidings, passing loop and connections with the Northwich branch or the main line. The former North Stafford Railway platform and sidings once occupied the area on the right of the picture now used as a car park.

On the approach to Goostrey station class 47 No 47463 with an unidentified train passes the site of a once extensive storage sidings to a Department of Transport and Industry oil storage terminal. Once occupied by Shellmex and BP it was operational from 1961 until 1974 with two Fowler 0-4-0 diesels for shunting. The sidings had been lifted only a short time before this picture was taken on 30th August 1987 all that remained was a single yard lamp.

The first Goostrey signal box was built by the LNWR in September 1891 and equipped with a 20-lever Tumbler frame. British Railways replaced it on 15th August 1954 by the box seen here, which is fitted with a 30-lever BR Standard 4½ inch frame. When electrification came on 8th June 1959 the box became a non-block post but remained in service until 19th October 1986, closing officially on 17th January 1988.

Goostrey station was in my view one of the most attractive and best-kept country stations situated on a busy main line. This picture, taken in July 1987, shows the main station building on the Manchester-bound platform. It still retained a booking office, Porter's rooms, waiting rooms and toilets and I am reliably informed it had changed very little in appearance from the time it was constructed by the M&BR in 1842.

When this picture was taken in July 1987 the Crewe-Bound platform had no original station infrastructure or passenger waiting facilities, just a 'bus' type enclosed waiting shelter. However, in amongst the well cared for flower beds, pointed out to me by one of the station staff, was a piece of M&BR history-a carved piece of stone which commemorated the building of Holmes Chapel and Chelford viaducts by the railway engineer George Watson Buck in 1841. The stone was unearthed by a local railwayman and placed on show at the station in the early 1980s. Some years later, in the face of o good deal of local controversy, it was relocated to a nearby garden centre where I believe it still resides.

On 12th August 1984 engineering operations in the Stoke area required Manchester trains to be diverted via Stockport and Crewe and seen here at Goostrey is IC125 set working the 0915hrs Exeter-Manchester Piccadilly.

A warm summer Sunday afternoon at Goostrey as class 47 No 47551 with 87021 and the 1445hrs Manchester Piccadilly in tow provides an interesting spectacle to the young onlookers as the ensemble rushes by.

There is no doubt that Goostrey station is situated in a quiet rural location and on occasions a passing train interrupts that peace. However on Sunday 31st July 1983 the passing train was a little more noisy as class 40 No 40080 with 85009 and its unidentified train of eight Mk1 bogies in tow thunder through the station at an attention-grabbing speed.

Lots of engineering operations on the North Stafford route between Stoke and Macclesfield meant that trains would be diverted via the M&BR line. On 17th September 1989 there seemed to be more than usual and motive power came in various classes as seen here at Goostrey with class 31s No's 31467 and 31450 heading towards Crewe with an unidentified train.

Another heavyweight at Goostrey on 24th July 1983 with class 40 No 40126 making light work of the diverted 1425hrs Manchester Piccadilly-Paddington. Of course 40126 became world famous after it was hijacked during The Great Train Robbery in August 1962. Its fame (or infamy) did not save it from the cutting torch however and it was scrapped at Crewe in 1986.

On 15th November 1986 two newly refurbished class 309 EMUs worked the 'Network Exile' railtour from Euston to Hadfield, providing the very first sighting of this class in Network livery north of Wolverton. Units 309611/15 are seen here heading through Goostrey proving that even EMUs can provide interesting stock for railtours. (As I recall the train was packed!)

The 14th of May 1988 was, I recollect, one of those delightful early summer Saturdays, not a cloud in the sky and I was content that the train I had come to photograph was running to time. There was a brief moment of concern however when the local constabulary stopped to enquire why I was perched on top of a gatepost! "Waiting to photograph a train," I told him; "a steam train?" he asked - "no a couple of diesel engines" I replied. He pondered for a moment and with one eyebrow raised said "Oh" and then drove off. A few minutes later class 50s No's 50009 and 50036 improved the scene even more as they thundered across Chelford Viaduct with the 'Hoover Dambuster' railtour.

3: SANDBACH – MIDDLEWICH – NORTHWICH

In anticipation of goods traffic and the possibility of large quantities of salt being extracted from deposits found beneath the Northwich area, the LNWR applied for Parliamentary approval to build a line between Sandbach and Northwich. Authorisation was given in1863 for an 8.75-mile, mostly single-track railway between the two towns and it opened to freight traffic in November 1867. Passenger trains started from Sandbach on 1st July 1868 calling at an intermediate halt at Cledford Bridge, a station at Middlewich and a Halt at Billinge Green situated midway between Middlewich and Northwich. At its peak eight Crewe-Northwich trains and nine return workings each day, Monday to Saturday, served the line including three London Euston-Liverpool trains (and returns), which did not stop at the halts. The halts closed in 1942 as 'Wartime Economy Measures' and the line closed completely to passengers on 4th January 1960. In 1967 the line closed to regular freight traffic with the exception of occasional trains that served the private sidings of Murgatroyds Chemicals near Sandbach and British Salt works at Cledford. This chapter however illustrates the variety of traffic using the line as a diversionary route during the 1980s.

When it was realised that the class 45/0 'Peaks' were soon to be phased out, these locomotives became the centre of attention for enthusiasts and were being requested for various railtours. On 6th June 1987, 45029 is seen here in charge of Hertfordshire Railtours the 'Hills & Cities Tour' negotiating Sandbach Junction to join the freight only branch to Northwich.

A view of Sandbach Junction with the branch to Middlewich and Northwich seen swinging away to the left of the Crewe-Manchester main line. Sandbach station is in fact more than a mile from the town centre at the village of Elworth and the bridge visible in the background carries the A533 Sandbach-Middlewich road.

A Centenary special for the *Lancashire Evening Post* from Euston to Morecambe covered some unusual territory on 23rd November 1986, when the train was diverted from the West Coast Mainline at Crewe. Class 47 No 47459 is seen here passing the ICI Chemical Works (former 'Murgatroyds' works) sidings near Sandbach with the VSOE Pullmans heading towards Northwich. The works is now Albion Inorganic Chemicals and still has an active rail connection.

From Sandbach Junction the line is double track as far as 'Murgatroyds' Junction and thereafter is singled until Middlewich where double track is restored through the station site to form a passing loop. On the single line section near to the British Salt Works at Cledford, class 47/3 No 47332 ambles towards Northwich with an unidentified train, diverted from the West Coast Main Line on 14th February 1988.

Whenever the weekend diversions took place over this particular line, information on the actual sequence of trains was limited so it made identification of trains very difficult. Sunday 14th February 1988 was no exception when an unusual combination appeared in the form of class 47/1 No 47198 with class 31/1 No 31460 and an unidentified northbound train, seen here entering the double track at Middlewich.

Platform edges at Middlewich station were still intact on 21st June 1988 as class 37/8 No 37802 (CF) trundles through with a rake of Cawoods PFAs. Built by Standard Wagon Co in 1986/87 Cawoods had 160 of these dropped-floor container wagons primarily for export coal traffic from Ellington Colliery, South Wales to their terminal at Ellesmere Port. In order to carry 8'6" containers and keep within loading gauge the wagons were fitted with small wheels. In the distance is an unidentified class 31 running light-engine towards Northwich. *(Peter Thorley)*

Looming out of the morning mist on 26th April 1986 class 45/1 No 45121 with Inter City Pullman stock slows at Middlewich station to rejoin the single line to Northwich whilst working the 'Pennine Summits Pullman' railtour.

On 13th April 1983 class 40 No 40028 ambles along the Northwich branch with a train of TTB chemical tanks probably originating from the ICI works. The ensemble is seen here just north of Middlewich crossing the bridges spanning Whatcroft Hall Lane and the Trent and Mersey Canal.

It was a bitterly cold day at Davenham Bridge as an unidentified class 47 and its train make a surprise appearance as they head south past the fishing pools at unusually high speed on Sunday 14th December 1986.

A sylvan setting for class 45/0 45029 and its train, the 'Hills & Cities Tour', seen here passing through the cutting at Davenham as they make steady progress towards Northwich on 6th June 1987.

Network SouthEast liveried class 47/4 No 47583 'County of Herefordshire' (SF) heads north through Rudheath with an unidentified Euston-Liverpool service on Sunday 14th December 1986.

On Sunday 7th December 1986, class 47/6 No 47646 with an unidentified train diverted from the West Coast Main Line (WCML) arrives at Northwich South Junction to take the westbound track to Northwich West Junction. The line in the foreground heads east to Northwich Station Junction.

The same day and the same train as it rounds the curve to Northwich West Junction. Here the train will connect with the old Cheshire Lines Committee Manchester-Chester line, (out of sight in front of the row of houses). The train will then run for a short distance before rejoining the WCML at Hartford Junction.

4: ASHLEY – NORTHWICH – CHESTER

This line is very interesting, pure Cheshire Lines Committee (CLC) throughout but it has a complicated beginning that, space permitted, cannot be explained fully here. Suffice to say though, the line opened in stages starting with Altrincham to Knutsford on 12th May 1862; Knutsford to Northwich 1st January 1863 and through to Chester, in stages again, between 1st September 1869 and 2nd November 1874 when the line was concluded at Chester Northgate. This chapter illustrates the line between Ashley and Chester, focusing mainly on Northwich, which, because of its underlying mineral deposits, was one of the main reasons for the railway's presence. The Northwich Salt Branches alone accounted for over 5 miles of independent railway in the area. Northwich Shed lingered on well into the 1980s and it receives well-deserved coverage.

I guess that Sir Nigel Gresley would not have objected to his namesake being stabled at Northwich Shed, particularly when the locomotive was taking part in the 'Rocket 150' celebrations at Rainhill. The shed was in remarkably clean condition, as was his A4 No 4498, when this picture was taken in the early evening of 5th May 1980.

Little had changed at Ashley station when this picture was taken on 24th March 1989 as class 108/2 DMU (CH250) departs with an afternoon Chester-Manchester service. The station house (under private ownership) was in surprisingly good condition and the platform shelter appeared to be unchanged from when the CLC built it - even retaining its wooden fire bucket rack.

During the 1980s when steam operations were banned from electrified routes this line was a favourite with railtour operators and enthusiasts. On 24th March 1989 Ex LMS 'Black Five' No 5407 makes a fine sight as she takes the gradient between Ashley and Mobberley whilst working 'The Lancastrian' railtour.

On the same day, following the steam special, one of the line's regular performers, a Tunstead-Northwich limestone train headed by class 37/6 No's 37682 and 37683. I believe this one was the weekdays-only 7F45, 1330hrs Tunstead (Great Rocks)-ICI Lostock Works Northwich.

Not all steam specials were run for enthusiasts and in some cases not run to a budget either as this train demonstrates. It was Saturday 29th September 1984 as Ex LNER A3 No 4472 'Flying Scotsman' storms the bank between Mobberley and Knutsford with a rake of Pullmans whilst working the 'Wilsons Brewery 150th Anniversary Special'.

The Cheshire Lines Committee opened Knutsford East signal box on 27th March 1886 but interestingly to a Stevens design with a Stevens' 20-lever frame. The box, seen here on 8th July 1989, was situated at the east end of the Chester-bound platform and it remained in use until closure on 20th October 1996.

This is a general view of Knutsford Station during the summer of 1984 with almost the entire infrastructure intact except that the canopies to the main platform buildings have been removed. Semaphore signals are still in use at that time as is the crossover and ground signal dolly.

This is a similar view to the above photograph, taken 8th July 1990, with the ornate CLC designed cast iron supports and canopy on the Manchester-bound side with newly ballasted track following removal of the crossover. The class 108 DMU is working an early evening Manchester-Chester service.

A twin-lens reflex Rolliecord 1b, 120 roll film camera was used for this photograph. It produced very good pictures but was awkward to capture moving trains. When I was told about the steam special I thought I would give the camera a go and I would take my trusty Nikon as back-up. Unfortunately I had used up all my 120 stock except for a roll of Ilford FP4 that expired in June 1967, more than a year before the end of steam on BR!! It still got the picture though - Ex LMS 4-6-2 No 6201 'Princess Elizabeth' passing Plumley in February 1986 as she worked 'The White Rose' railtour.

On Saturday 21st February 1987 class 142 DMU No 142054 arrives at Plumley station with the 1328 Chester-Manchester Piccadilly service. The semaphore signal on the left I believe was a CLC post and mechanism with a BR design arm attached.

Looking in the direction of Northwich, this is a general view of Plumley station taken on the 21st February 1987. It shows the grand style of architecture in which the CLC built their country stations. Unfortunately by this date it was abandoned, un-staffed and the station house boarded up.

A year later, on Saturday 26th March 1988, the waiting shelter seen on the left of the above picture was gone and bramble was starting to take over the platform. This sorry sight however would probably have not have attracted the attention of the football supporters on board the 'Footex' to Manchester as it raced through the station behind class 47/4 No 47479.

Another sorry sight on 21st February 1987 and facing east was Lostock Gralam station. Almost identical in style and proportions to Plumley station it was also in an identical un-staffed and derelict condition.

August 1983 and class 25 No's 25044 and 25059 leave ICI's Lostock Works sidings at Northwich and head west towards Northwich Station Junction with a train of empty coal wagons. *(Peter Rawlins)*

A view looking east from the island platform steps at Northwich station as a class 108 DMU prepares to depart with the 1428 Chester-Manchester Oxford Road service on Thursday 5th February 1987. The CLC constructed the platform as an island to share with LNWR trains arriving from the Sandbach-Northwich branch. The lines on the right connect (and still do) with Northwich Station Junction and the current freight-only line to Sandbach.

A view looking in the opposite direction at Northwich station on Sunday 7th December 1986 as class 142 'Pacer' DMU No 142002 waits to depart with the 1433 Manchester Piccadilly-Chester. Northwich was an important junction to the CLC and the station reflects this status with highly decorative canopy, cast iron supports and a clock, which would not look out of place at a main line terminus. Interestingly the clock is now the subject of a restoration scheme and there is a local initiative currently bidding for funds.

Northwich Shed was a 6-road dead end structure built in 1869 and served a huge variety of steam and diesel locomotives until 1985 when it finally closed. This picture was taken on 7th December 1986 and by that date some of the track had already been recovered from the yard and sidings and during the following 12 months the site was cleared.

Twenty-two years later and the scene as changed completely with the shed area now occupied by a housing development but with road names that at least acknowledge its railway heritage. The station building has not changed in appearance but some of the rooms are now in use as retail outlets. 22nd April 2008.

In complete contrast to the previous picture, this is Northwich shed in happier times as class 24 No 24081, in company with BR Standard class 4 2-6-4T No 80079, makes an appearance at an open day in May 1980. There was a lot of activity at that time due to the shed's participation in the 'Rocket 150' celebrations when a number of visiting engines were temporarily stabled and prepared here.

The unmistakable atmosphere of a locomotive shed is evident here as class 40 No 40057 stands in the shed at Northwich while waiting its next turn of duty in August 1983. *(Peter Rawlins)*

Ex-Southern Railway 4-6-0 No 850 'Lord Nelson' is a long way from home on 12th June 1981 as it is being prepared for one of the frequent Trans Pennine Pullman specials that operated during the early 1980s. For these particular charters No 850 hauled the train from Northwich to Leeds or vice versa.

August 1983 and class 40 No 40047 drifts through the station towards Hartford Junction with a long train of CSA/CSV Ash Hoppers. On the right a coal train passes by on the line to Northwich Station Junction and at the left of the picture work is in progress to remove track from the Down sidings and station goods yard, which is now occupied by a large Tesco store, filling station and car park.

As the line became more popular with steam tour operators the motive power was varied to maintain interest. Saturday 15th June produced good weather and a fine spectacle at Delamere as BR class 9f 2-10-0 No 92220 'Evening Star' storms past with a York to Shrewsbury special. Although some people decided that it was ok to 'picnic' at the line side, I was safely on the other side of the fence!

Not to be upstaged completely by the 9f, while there was still spectators around, class 47/4 No 47445 was hot on the special's heels as it trundled through Delamere station on 15th June 1985 with an unidentified MGR train.

Four years later and another steam special takes to the Delamere Forest as rebuilt Merchant Navy class 4-6-2 No 35028 'Clan Line' rushes through Delamere station on 27th May 1989 with a special charter to the Heritage Centre at Crewe.

This is Chester General on 21st September 1985 as brand new class 142 'Pacer' DMU No 142003 departs the station. Although the class 142s were about to replace the ageing class 108 units on the Manchester service this particular set was actually leaving the Wrexham and Bidston bay whilst working a trial run to Bidston. *(Peter Thorley)*

5: CREWE – CHESTER

Royal Assent was given by Queen Victoria to in-corporate a new railway company, the Chester & Crewe Railway (C&CR), on 30th June 1837. This happened just four days before the Grand Junction Railway (GJR) opened its line and newly built station at Crewe. The 21-mile line to Chester, which was surveyed originally by George Stevenson as part of a proposed route through to Holyhead, was opened on 1st October 1840-just four months after the C&CR was absorbed by the GJR. From the outset the line served no significant areas of population and during the years 1952 to 1966 the five intermediate stations were closed, the last being Beeston Castle & Tarporley. The line remains open however as a busy route for freight traffic and passenger trains working through to Chester and North Wales. This chapter gives an idea of the variety of trains that worked this line in the 1980s, a decade that brought an abundance of special trains to the area and some of these are illustrated in the following pages.

On 26th September 1984 a 4-car class 120 DMU set leaves platform 3a with an afternoon service to Chester with re-numbered unit M54335 in the lead. Standing in platform 4a is class 309 EMU No 309011 having just arrived from Liverpool. In less than 12 months, following the station's remodelling, the Crewe-Liverpool EMU's would be required to swap platforms because platform 4a (now platform 9) was to be lengthened and connected to the Chester line only.

Sunday 11th August 1991 witnessed some 'serious' haulage out of Crewe with six special trains double headed by classes 20, 37, 56, 58 and 60. This exceptional day was sponsored by Trainload Coal to help raise funds for Cerebral Palsy victim Leanna Davies to receive treatment at the Peto Institute, Poland. One such train, the 1540hrs Crewe-Llandudno is seen here behind Coal Sector class 58s No 58007 and 58003, with 6,600-horse power on tap, just picking up speed after passing Crewe Works.

British Rail Engineering Ltd (BREL) held an open day on 21st July 1990 and on this same day there were a number of regular steam-hauled services running to North Wales. One of these is shown here headed by Ex-LNER 4-6-2 No 4472 *Flying Scotsman* as it passes the Pyms Lane factory of Rolls Royce Motors.

Ex-Southern Railway rebuilt West Country 4-6-2 No 34027 *'Taw Valley'* heads towards Chester on 16th August 1989 whilst working a Crewe-North Wales Coast Express. The train is about to cross the Middlewich Branch of the Shropshire Union Canal at Venetian Marina. *(Peter Thorley)*

It is early evening at New Aston Hall as Ex-LNER A4 pacific No 60009 *'Union of South Africa'* heads the return working of an earlier Crewe Heritage Centre-Llandudno steam special on 8th July 1990.

On 19th July 1989 class 47/1 No 47150 rushes towards Crewe, past the old Worleston station (now a private dwelling), with a Holyhead-Lawley Street Freightliner train. The station closed following the Beeching Report, which proposed that the Crewe-Chester line should remain open but local stopping services were not viable and should be discontinued.

New Aston Hall again as Ex Southern Railway rebuilt West Country 4-6-2 No 34027 *'Taw Valley'* drifts by with a return working of a North Wales Coast Express on Sunday 15th July 1990.

The next few photographs are taken around Wardle Bank, which I found to be an excellent vantage point for trains on this part of the line. Unfortunately the passage of time has resulted in the view now being obscured by trees and shrubbery. On 24th June 1990 the view is clear (except for steam and smoke!) as Ex-BR 4-6-2 No 71000 *'Duke of Gloucester'* speeds past with a Crewe Heritage Centre steam special to Llandudno.

On Saturday 21st April 1984 at Wardle Bank class 25 No 25284 makes light work of nine 'Sea Cow' bogie ballast wagons as it coasts past towards Chester.

After a number of reliability problems on the 'Pennine Forty' railtour a few weeks before, the National Collection's class 40 No 40122 is seen here on 2nd April 1988 in fine fettle as she storms past Wardle Bank in a new coat of 'Museum' green with small yellow warning panel. 40122 took Hertfordshire Rail Tours *'The Tubular Belle'* charter train to Llandudno, Holyhead (twice) and Blaenau Ffestiniog.

The revival of steam on this particular line started in 1988 when a new facility at the Crewe Heritage Centre, which opened the previous year, enabled main-line steam locomotives to be stabled and serviced there. On 21st August 1988 the first of many steam-hauled passenger excursions along this route commenced with Ex-LMS 4-6-2 No 6201 *'Princess Elizabeth'* carrying the Crewe Heritage Centre name-board seen here at Wardle Bank on that inaugural run.

For a second time in six weeks the Chester line accommodated class 50 power as 50007 *'Sir Edward Elgar'* is seen here rushing through Wardle Bank with the 'Conway Crusader II' railtour to Blaenau Ffestiniog on 21st April 1984.

In the 1980s Crewe-Holyhead trains were regularly loco-hauled and an example is seen here on 14th June 1983 passing Wardle Bank with class 47 No 47563 in charge of the 1102hrs Crewe-Holyhead service.

A warm summer morning enhances the deeply rural nature of the Crewe-Chester line on 14th June 1983, as class 47 No 47588 is seen here passing Tweedale Bridge with the 0815 Holyhead-Crewe.

During its lifetime Calveley station had two signal boxes, the first of which opened c1870. The second box, opened in 1901, was built by the LNWR and fitted with their 30-lever Tumbler frame. The box remained in use until closure on 15th August 1982 and is pictured here on 4th December 1982. *(Peter Thorley)*

As class 150 'Sprinter' units began to replace the ageing class 120 and 118 DMUs some of the loco-hauled Crewe–Holyhead diagrams were substituted with new class 150/2 sets. One of these workings is seen here as 4-car set No 150223 passes Tilstone Bank near Tarporley with a late afternoon Crewe–Holyhead service on 28th June 1987.

Two years later class 108 Derby Lightweight DMUs were still in charge of most of the Crewe–Chester 'locals'. On 19th July 1989 one of these 2-car sets, CH268, is seen here at Beeston Brook with an unidentified working to Llandudno.

Beeston Castle & Tarporley on 4th February 1987 as class 47 No 47194 picks its way past the old station sidings with two brand new 'Merseyrail' class 508 EMU sets bound for the new Wirral Line at Liverpool.

No less than three different Beeston Castle & Tarporley signal boxes were built here. Unfortunately no details of the first box survive but the 2nd box opened c1883 and was equipped with a LNWR 19-lever Tumbler frame. This was subsequently demolished and replaced in 1901 with a new structure fitted with a LNWR 26-lever Tappet frame. This signal box, seen here on 4th February 1987, survives and is still in use.

Just passing Bates Mill Lane on 28th June 1987 class 47/5, No 47555 *'The Commonwealth Spirit'*, complete with snowploughs and Network Southeast stock, proceeds at some haste towards Crewe.

At Chester General station on 10th October 1985 class 37s No 37092 and 37058 drift through with a rake of Peakstone Hoppers, destination unknown. At that time some rationalisation was already being carried out with one of the siding roads having been isolated.

Class 47/3 No 37344 passes through Chester General station in the early afternoon of 10th October 1985 with a substantial train of parcels and newspaper vans in tow. In the background a class 118/2 DMU stands in the Manchester bay.

Class 47/5 No 47575 *'City of Hereford'* stands at platform 3 ready to depart with the 1305hrs Holyhead-Euston on 10th October 1985.

A view of Chester Motive Power Depot on Saturday 10th March 1984 where several classes of DMU are seen stabled over that weekend in the 1957-built diesel depot, on the washing racks and behind the old steam shed. Class 40 No 40104 takes a rest by the side of the DMUs. Sadly all of this is now consigned to history.

An industrial steam locomotive standing by the old turntable at Chester Northgate Shed (or what was left of it) created a bit of interest on 10th March 1984. I discovered later that it is a Peckett W6 class 0-4-0ST, works number 1990, built in 1940 for the Central Electricity Generating Board's Ironbridge power station, Shropshire. It was then named *Ironbridge No 3* and is currently in preservation at Telford.

6: CREWE – NANTWICH – WRENBURY – WHITCHURCH

On 20th August 1853 the Shrewsbury & Crewe Railway was authorised by Parliament to build a 32½-mile line to connect the two towns. Five years elapsed before the line was opened (by the LNWR) on 1st September 1858. Some of this delay was due to political intervention and time spent by the contractors in acquiring some of the line they needed to enter Shrewsbury station. The line has always been a busy one with through services from South Wales with regular GWR action into Crewe and the celebrated 'Pines Express' from Manchester to Bournemouth West. It was still busy in the 1980s and the following pictures illustrate a variety of motive power and some of the infrastructure on the section between Crewe and Whitchurch.

In 1981 class 25s worked most of the Crewe-Cardiff trains and then gradually class 33s started to take over some of these diagrams. On a Saturday afternoon in early May 1981 class 25 No 25224 had just arrived in the 'Salop' bay, platform 4b, at Crewe and is about to be uncoupled from the train and then undertake the run round.

On the same day station shunter 08737 is about to draw the stock clear from platform 4b so that the 25 can run out of the platform. The 25 returns to couple up again as soon as the 08 completes its manoeuvre. Cardiff trains invariably comprised 5 Mk1 Western Region coaches. The class 86 AC electric is standing in Bank Engine Siding waiting its next turn of duty.

August 1983 and class 33021 is seen here departing platform 5b in charge of an unidentified afternoon train to Cardiff. The train will proceed from here to Crewe South Junction before swinging right onto the Shrewsbury line. *(Peter Rawlins)*

August 1983 again when a pair of class 33s surprised the photographer at Gresty Lane as they headed onto the Shrewsbury line with an unidentified railtour. The lead engine was 33018, unfortunately during the mild confusion, the second loco's number was not taken. *(Peter Rawlins)*

For a several months during late 1986 and early 1987 a number of condemned locomotives were stored at Gresty Lane Sidings. On 21st February 1987 a contingent of class 25s appeared consisting of 25089, 25230, 25196, 25324 and 25285. Behind them on the next line were two other locos, 25042 and 97405 (40060) *'Ancient Mariner'*.

Gresty Lane No1 signal box has been known variously as Gresty Lane Junction, Gresty Lane Sidings and Gresty Lane Goods until 1928 when the current name was adopted. The first box opened in 1870, which lasted until the present structure was built in 1899 and fitted with a 66-lever Crewe Panel Frame. This was replaced with a new 90-switch panel over a 2-day closure on 26/27th November 1978 and it is still operational today.

Another view of Gresty Lane No 1 signal box, taken on 9th December 1984, this time showing its central position within the apex of the junction. In the foreground are the tracks from West Sidings that join (at the left of the picture) with the Shrewsbury line, which is out of sight behind the signal box. The buildings in the left background are the old Permanent Way Works.

Gresty Lane No2 signal box was the next cabin towards Shrewsbury and was opened on 24th September 1928 and equipped with a LNWR 19-lever Tappet Frame. In my view it was the classic signal cabin design, complete with outside loo! Unfortunately it was closed on 28th October 1984, ahead of the re-signalling at Crewe and demolished the following year on 1st December 1985. There were sidings both sides of the main line here and the single line on the right leads into a permanent way yard.

Climbing away from Gresty Lane is ex-Southern Railway, (BR-rebuilt) West Country 4-6-2 No 34027 *'Taw Valley'* heading towards Willaston with *'The West Mercian'* railtour on 20th May 1989.

I have included this photograph as a classic example of being 'unprepared for the unexpected' that normally results in a picture that tells half a story! In June 1990, whilst waiting at Willaston for a steam special from Shrewsbury, two Trainload Metals class 37s stormed out of the blue and this is the result - and I didn't even get both numbers. 37518 is at the rear and the train consisted of a number of BDAs carrying steel blooms, destination unknown.

The station at Willaston was closed in December 1954 but the original signal box dating from 1870 remained. This picture, taken on 9th December 1984, shows the replacement BR (LMR) box opened on 10th December 1958 and fitted with a LMR Standard '4½ inch' 30-lever frame. Following the centralised signalling of Crewe this box was demolished on 15th December 1985.

An early evening in July 1983 and class 47 No 47316 heads out of Willaston towards Nantwich with 2 GUVs and a Mk1 parcels van for Shrewsbury. *(Peter Rawlins)*

A view of Nantwich station crossing showing the signal box and manually operated crossing gates, pedestrian picket gates and, bottom right, the original wrought iron footbridge steps. 7th June 1982.

The Nantwich signalman stands proudly by the wheel that operates the manual gates protecting the crossing over the A530 Whitchurch Road. This signal box is the last of three boxes to be built here and it was opened by the LMS on 25th April 1948. When this photograph was taken on 8th June 1982 it was in almost original condition except that the 30-lever REC Frame had a number of redundant levers.

A view of Nantwich station signal box from the footbridge with the manual crossing gates closed for class 40 No 40001 heading for Gresty Lane with a ballast train, watched by two elderly pedestrians waiting to cross. 7th June 1982.

Class 120 DMUs were regular performers on the Crewe-Shrewsbury locals and a 3-car set is seen calling at Nantwich at 1347hrs on 14th June 1983 with a Shrewsbury-Crewe working. By this date the station buildings were not in use.

Looking in the direction of Wrenbury this is a view of the station showing the original wrought iron footbridge built in 1870 by the LNWR. The extra-tall double home/ starter signal allows drivers an advance view as the line approaches on quite a severe curve. Class 25 No 25194 ambles along light engine towards Crewe on 14th June 1983.

In ex-works condition class 47 No 47361 is seen here passing through Nantwich with the Crewe Works Test Train heading back to the works after a test run on 14th June 1983. Nantwich achieved junction status in October 1863 when the Great Western Railway (GWR) opened its line to Market Drayton and Wellington (1867) thus giving the GWR a through route south from Crewe. Following the Beeching recommendations the line closed on 9th September 1963.

The sharp curve into the station can be seen here as class 40 No 40096 runs through the station with empty ballast wagons to Coton Hill CEE sidings, Shrewsbury on 7th June 1982.

An almost perfect summer morning 7th June 1982 brought Class 40 No 40001 out into the sunshine at Wrenbury whilst working another Crewe-Coton Hill Sidings ballast train empties.

Almost the same spot on the same day class 25/1 No 25168 has clear signals through Wrenbury with the usual 5-coach train working the 1105 Crewe-Cardiff.

Class 108/1 power-twin set arrives at Wrenbury with the 1320 Crewe-Shrewsbury on 8th June 1982. The station buildings are still occupied and in private ownership.

On the same day a slightly re-styled class 108/2 two-car DMU slows for a stop at Wrenbury with a late morning Shrewsbury-Crewe service.

During the early 1980s class 25 duties on Crewe-South Wales services began to diminish as Southern Region class 33s started to take over these diagrams. On 7th June 1982 class 33/0 No 33050 makes light work of its 5-coach train as it approaches Wrenbury with the 0940hrs Cardiff-Crewe.

Wrenbury Signal box was opened by the LNWR in January 1876 and equipped with their own design 20-lever Tumbler Frame. It did not however become a block post until February 1882. The box is still in use today but 3 levers were taken out of use in 1992 after (I understand) a crossover was removed. To make the picture complete, class 33/0 No 33016 breezes past with 1140hrs Cardiff-Crewe service.

Most of the lines in Cheshire have all the attributes of the country railway and this picture is typical of the rural setting between Wrenbury and Whitchurch. Class 37/4 No 37427 requires just a tad of regulator for its load of two GUVs heading for the sorting depot at Shrewsbury on 20th February 1988. *(Peter Thorley)*

Although we are just outside the boundary of Cheshire it seemed appropriate to end this chapter at Whitchurch. It was once an important junction with the Cambrian Railway Co who made a connection here with their line from Oswestry and Ellesmere on 27th July 1864. This line however closed on 23rd November 1964 but the Shrewsbury line survived and seen here at Whitchurch on 28th March 1985 is a class 120 DMU with a 'local' bound for Crewe. *(Peter Thorley)*

7: CREWE LOCOMOTIVE WORKS

The Grand Junction Railway opened its first locomotive works at Crewe in September 1843, at a site just north of the station, known later as the 'Old Works'. This chapter however looks at the locomotive works that most people are familiar with – the very large site located between the Chester line and West Street. The Works here was intensely developed from 1854 until the 1920s when the new erecting shops were built at the extreme west end of the Works. By 1900 Crewe Locomotive Works had become world famous when in March of that year the 4000th engine was built at Crewe, a 4-cylinder Compound 4-4-0 No 1926 'La France'. During the late 1960s as steam was withdrawn the Works was adapted to build and repair diesel and electric locomotives. During the early 1980s little of this work had changed and the layout of the Works was much the same as it was during steam days, except that the Steel Works or 'Melts' had been converted to a locomotive scrap shed. Also, new locomotives were still being built; class 56, class 43 (HST Power Cars), Class 87/2 and class 91 (Electra) together with overhauls and repairs undertaken on almost every type of diesel and electric locomotive. This chapter is a personal record of the various visits I made to the Works, from 1981 to 1990. For those readers not familiar with the 'Sunday' guided tours, I have set out the first 36 pictures in the order of 'the tour' starting from Park Entrance. The final pictures are a selection from 3 Open Days.

This is one of the four cast iron eagles, which adorned the corner pillars of 'Eagle Bridge' that spanned the Chester line with a rail connection to the Carriage Works and Repair Shops, which is now the site of the Electric Depot. It is widely held that they were found amongst scrap being delivered to the smelter but the Steel Works manager rescued them precisely at the time the bridge was under construction. This particular 'Eagle' is at the entrance to the Electric Depot in Victoria Avenue and the others are situated at 'The Railway Age' entrance, North Junction Signal Box and outside the 'Eagle Bridge Health and Wellbeing Centre' in Dunwoody Way.

The Reception sidings are particularly full on 5th June 1983 with 45076 topped and tailed by 40073 and 40084 as they stand waiting for attention at the side of the Asbestos House.

Starting 'the tour' from Park Entrance the first locomotives in the Reception Sidings line-up are 40027 and 47457 standing at the side of the Traction Motor Shop. 5th June 1983.

Moving down the Reception Sidings, at the side of the old Electric Erecting Shop, class 40 No's 40145, 40034 and class 47, No 47343 stand waiting repairs. 5th June 1983.

On the same day a trio of 40s, No's 40180, 40183 and 40188 are lined up in the storage roads. It is thought that the building on the right is the old Copper Shop.

On 17th February 1985 the storage sidings have locomotives and various items of rolling stock that had been there for quite some time. Heading the line-up are 81015 and 40049 both of which were probably withdrawn from service.

August 1983 and class 47, No 47535 is in the Works for major repair following accident damage at an unknown incident. *(Peter Rawlins)*

The Storage Ground on 23rd March 1986 and six class 40s awaiting their fate in the scrap shed situated behind the camera. At the front are 40181 and 40020.

A grand view of Stone Yard Bank on 5th June 1983, taken from 'Eagle Bridge', with no less than 11 condemned class 40s in residence. Above the rear of the 40s is Flag Lane Bridge with the remains of the old 'Chester line' in the right foreground. The current Chester line is the other side of the wall and in the extreme upper right are the former carriage storage sheds. The locomotives are: 40006, 40008, and 40023 40065, 40088, 40101, 40115, 40136, 40138, 40139 and 40182.

On 17th February 1985 the line-up at Stone Yard Bank had changed a little but the numbers awaiting their fate were not diminished. The 40-metre high building in the background is the old Steel Works or 'Melts', then used as the scrapping shed and at the extreme middle left of the picture is 'Eagle Bridge'.

Looking particularly sun-bleached on 4th July 1987 class 40 No's 40195 and 40091 are at the head of the queue at the Storage Ground waiting to be moved into the scrap shed. By this date some of the tracks here had been lifted and it was looking more like an area to store waste materials. Compare this picture with that on page 109. *(Peter Thorley)*

This is Flag Lane signal box when photographed on 17th February 1985. In the background is Flag Lane Bridge with the old Chester line passing beneath although at that time the tracks came to an end just short of Chester Bridge. *(Peter Thorley)*

Photographed from almost the same position, this is the scene on 11th July 2008 with motor traffic travelling beneath Flag Lane Bridge that now spans the 'Dunwoody Way' connecting West Street with the town centre.

Flag Lane signal box was situated between Stone Yard Bank and Flag Lane Bridge controlling the web of lines into the Works. There was a signal box here from c1910 the one shown here was opened in 1963 and is a BR (LMR) Type 15 fitted with a 15-lever Tappet Frame The line on the immediate right of the picture ran directly into the Works, whereas a locomotive leaving the site would take the line seen climbing away towards the 'Melts', turning left over Eagle Bridge, through the Electric Depot and onto the Chester line.

Another view of the Storage Ground photographed on 23rd March 1986 when in fact a new track had been added. By this date the whole of the area was crammed with class 40s waiting for the cutters torch and the two nearest the camera are 40044 and 40150.

Inside the former Steel Works or 'Melts' class 40 No 40177 is in the early stages of being stripped down on 23rd March 1986.

Three years earlier on 5th June 1983 three other class 40s; 40103, 40064 and 40142 are meeting the same fate with a fresh supply of gas bottles at the ready. The wagon is not there for cutting up, but is probably waiting to be filled with non-ferrous material.

After the 'Melts' it was a bit more uplifting to go through the Paint Shop and see something that is returning to traffic having gone through the repair process and is being repainted. Seen here on 5th June 1983 is class 20 No 20029 with AC electric 81017 behind and, just visible on the left, class 86 No 86327.

For a number of years this class 45 No 45053 sat in a storage line at the side of the Test Bays and it is seen here on 5th February 1984.

At the front of the Traction Motor Shop another storage road accommodated class 40 No 40049, which I believe was still in service when this picture was taken on 5th June 1983.

Standing at the Brake Test Bay on 5th June 1983 was brand new class 56 No 56121 looking absolutely splendid in its large logo blue livery. In the background is part of 9 Shop.

Another view of the storage roads in front of the Traction Motor Shop with Class 40 No 40121 and class 20s; 20046, 20068 and 20176 waiting for attention in the works. 5th June 1983.

Outside the Test House on 23rd March 1986 is newly out-shopped class 47 No 47526, refinished in its large logo livery. Behind the loco, on the other side of the traverser, is 10 Shop.

On 23rd March 1986 Class 37 No 37425, looking almost new, stands at one of the Test Bays ready for a light trial run the following day. Behind the locomotive is the old Boiler Shop.

On the same day, across the other side of the traverser, another class 37 No 37505 stands outside 10 Shop after being turned out in 'Railfreight' grey. *(Peter Thorley)*

Inside the Works now in 10 Shop and at No 3 Bay, looking towards South Shop are AC electrics 87025 (left) and 86219 both undergoing repairs on 5th June 1983.

Standing in New Shop on 5th June 1983 class 81 No 81016 has been in the works since it was brought in on 9th December 1982 following an accident at Linslade, near Leighton Buzzard. The locomotive, built in March 1963 by AEI (BTH) Birmingham Railway & Carriage Works, was subsequently condemned and scrapped on the Works in 1985.

On 5th June 1983 Class 47 No 47231 heads a row of six of its class as they stand in No 2 Bay (10 Shop) receiving intermediate overhauls.

Unusual to find an 08 shunter parked inside the erecting shops and I speculate that it was not in for repair but had brought in a (unidentified) class 47 that was in various stages of primer. 23rd March 1986.

On 23rd March 1986 two class 85s No 85038 and 85016 were guests of No 3 Bay whilst undergoing repairs. 85038 was built at AEI/BR Doncaster Works in November 1963 and after 26 years service it was scrapped at MC Metals Glasgow in 1989.

When this picture was taken on 5th February 1984 the four locomotives seen here in 10 Shop for intermediate overhaul were still in traffic. Class 40s; 400224 (Lucania), 40027 (Parthia), 40030 (Scythia) and class 86 No 86221 (Vesta).

No 1 Bay in 10 Shop was equipped for New Work and seen here on 5th June 1983 is class 56 No 56127 under the early stages of construction.

At the far end of 10 Shop was a low-roofed area known as South Shop at the opposite side of the 'Old Traverser'. Seen here, on 23rd March 1986 is class 37 No 37210, minus its bogies, which are standing alongside on the parallel track.

This is the one and only class 89 to be built and it is seen here in 10 Shop on 23rd March 1986 at a very early stage in its build. It operated mostly on the East Coast Main Line and was named 'Avocet' on 16th September 1989. It became the test bed for the later class 91s until 1992 when a group of Brush Engineers purchased it only to be sold to GNER who returned it to traffic in 2000. It was subsequently purchased by the AC Locomotive Group and is currently at Barrow Hill.

A busy scene in 10 Shop on 5th June 1983 as New Work is underway with class 56 No 56125 in advance stage of construction alongside class 20 No 20096 which is receiving a major overhaul.

A view of New Shop on 17th February 1985 as newly painted class 20 No 20134 and unidentified class 47 wait for transfer to another part of the Works.

At the Park Entrance reception roads on 23 march 1986, newly out-shopped class 47 No 47449 has received the 'Crewe' treatment and looks almost new as she stands ready for a test run the following day.

This picture, taken on Sunday 17th February 1985, represents three pieces of the Works' history: the old 'Chester Line' at Flag Lane, the remains of the 'General Offices' (left), the 'Coppice' (right) and in my view the most iconic class of BR locomotives, ever-the class 40. In this line up are; (left) 40181, 40155, 40143, 40150, and 40104; (right) 40004 and 40195. It is ironic that almost all of the celebrated steam locomotives built in Crewe Works would have been photographed when new, here in this leafy glade.

Twenty-three years later, on Wednesday 6th February 2008, this picture was taken (give or take a few feet) from the same spot. The 40s and the track are long gone and the tree line has matured and part of the 'Coppice' was removed to accommodate a fast food franchise-and this is the access road to it – off Dunwoody Way.

WORKS OPEN DAY
6TH JUNE 1981

One of the locomotives that competed with Stevenson's *Rocket* at the Rainhill Trials in 1830 was Timothy Hackworth's *Sans Pareil*. Here at the Open Day is a marvellous working replica of that locomotive built by apprentices at the BR Shildon Works in the late 1970s. It is housed at the Timothy Hackworth Museum at Shildon and in May 1980 it took to the rails for the 'Rocket 150' celebrations at Rainhill. In 2000 it was relocated to Ironbridge where it underwent a full refit.

1981 had not been a very good year for the economy since it was in the middle of a recession. However this did not dampen the eagerness for enthusiasts to visit the Open Day. This view shows 9 Shop, the main 200-ton traverser and a complete but unpainted HST power car. The three chimney-like structures at the end of 9 Shop are exhaust stacks from the engine test bay.

At the south side of the traverser are the various storage, reception and test bay tracks leading to other parts of the Works. In 1981 the Open Day was very much about displaying the business of the Works and visiting 'showcase' locomotives was limited. On view here were newly-built HST power cars and class 47s in various stages of repair.

In 9 Shop was an area called the 'Blue Room' where locomotive power units were overhauled and in this view a Paxman Valenta engine from an HST power car is being checked out by a young enthusiast.

The main erecting shops appeared to be very busy as every 'rope' in 10 Shop had a number of locomotives at some stage of overhaul or repair. Class 47 No 47543 stands minus bogies and buffers as 37177 receives a bit of extra attention from a young enthusiast.

Further along 10 Shop and class 47 No 47280 stands behind another class 37 No 37209 both of which looked almost complete and had already been repainted and I would imagine that they were moved in here from the Paint Shop specifically for the Open Day.

At the time of the Open Day 9 Shop was populated with High Speed Train (HST) power cars. In this view are No's 43167 (nearest) and 43177. Both in fact were turned out as Driving Motor Luggage Vans (DMLVs).

A view of the Works looking south from the traverser, with New Shop on the right and, behind the class 47 is the old Boiler Shop, then used as the Frame Fabrication Shop.

Standing in one of the storage roads opposite the traverser is HST Driving Van Brake (DVB) No 43124 looking resplendent in its new IC 125 livery.

For a number of years AC electric class 84 No 84004 sat in a storage road outside New Shop and makes an interesting exhibit at the Open day. The locomotive was built in November 1960 by North British/GEC and was eventually scrapped at Crewe by A. Hampton & Co in 1988.

It is usual at an Open Day for a number of mainline locomotives to be made accessible for the public to see them at close-hand. Here class 47 No 47186 is being thoroughly checked out by a number of enthusiasts.

In front of class 47 No 47550 (complete with snow ploughs) is another product of Crewe Works, brand new HST (DVB) No 43165, which had been allocated to the Western Region to form part of a 9-car North East-South West cross country set. The building behind is New Shop.

WORKS OPEN DAY 2ND JUNE 1984

Three years on and the Works operated under the auspices of British Rail Engineering Limited (BREL) a separate commercial arm of British Rail. However, business was running as usual with new work in the form of AC electric Class 87/2 locomotives. Standing in 9 Shop is the first of this new class, No 87201 in its final stages of construction.

The 1984 Open Day I would suggest was a more interesting event, particularly for people who don't claim to be 'railway enthusiasts'. One large item of interest is seen here, BR Standard 4-6-2 No 71000 *'Duke of Gloucester'* that was certainly an attention grabber.

Standing in one of the reception roads is the National Collection's class 40 No 40122 or D200 as it was known prior to TOPS. At this time the locomotive was in general traffic but had recently undergone an overhaul and was turned out in its original British Railways green.

Across the tracks from D200, inside the Frame Fabrication Shop, is another Class 87/2 locomotive in its very early stages of construction. Unfortunately there was no indication as to the loco's identity.

Another interesting visitor was class 52 'Western' No D1041 *'Western Prince'* carrying the headboard 'The Extravaganza Special'. The locomotive is owned and operated by the Bury Transport Museum and insurance company Provident Mutual commercially sponsored its visit to Crewe.

Ex-LMS 8f 2-8-0 No 48151 is in light steam and attracting lots of visitors to the footplate. 48151 was allocated to Northwich Shed prior to it being withdrawn in 1968 and became an early example of steam locomotive passed for mainline operation. Four years after this event 48151 would return to Crewe for the opening of the Crewe Heritage Centre in July 1987.

Napier power at Crewe, in the form of English Electric Type 5 'Deltic' No D9000 (55022) *'Royal Scots Grey'*, is the centre of attention. These locomotives virtually took over the East Coast Main Line services as steam traction ended. All the Deltics were officially withdrawn on 4th January 1982 but there are several of the type in preservation, some of which are passed for mainline operation.

More steam, this time in the form of ex-LMS 'Princess Royal' class 4-6-2 No 6201 *'Princess Elizabeth'* again attracting a lot of attention from both the young and old enthusiast alike. These locomotives were introduced in 1933 for mainline passenger services on the West Coast Main Line and for a number of years No 6201 operated from Crewe North Shed (5A).

Standing just north of the Asbestos House another interesting visitor to the Open Day is Type 2 diesel D5054 (24054). This locomotive is owned by the Bury Transport Museum and currently operates on the East Lancs Railway at Bury.

WORKS OPEN DAY 21ST JULY 1990

By 1990 Crewe Locomotive Works was undertaking a number of 'good housekeeping' measures and the construction of new locomotives had diminished to just the class 91 'Electra'. The Open day however attracted a few unusual exhibits, one of which was this Network Southeast class 322 EMU, which operates on the Stansted Express service.

With the demand for locomotive construction in short supply and general maintenance work being carried out at the diesel Depots, Crewe Works took on all manner of external maintenance work, even road vehicles were brought into the plant for a while. In this view, an Army Maintenance Unit 'Vanguard' 0-4-0 diesel shunter No 254SU looks in fine condition after receiving a major overhaul. It stands here in a somewhat 'sanitised' 10 Shop.

Some of the very last locomotives to be built at Crewe Works were the class 91 'Electra' which were destined for work on the East Coast Main Line. This particular one, No 91024, is seen here in 10 Shop suspended by four Matterson Jacks. Normally a locomotive would be lifted and moved around the shop by overhead crane but these jacks, normally used at traction maintenance depots, were being used more regularly on the Works.

On this particular Open Day, provision was also made for a narrow gauge operation and seen here outside South Shop is Sandy River & Rangeley Lakes 15" gauge 2-6-2 locomotive built by the Fairbourne Railway in 1990. The loco is currently in service at the Cleethorpes Coast Railway, Lincolnshire.

Crewe Heritage Centre's class 47 No 47192 is turned out in fine condition and is seen here in a two-tone green livery with small yellow warning panel and carrying its original pre-TOPS number, D1842. It also sports a '5A' plate for Crewe North Shed.

Another example of the extraordinary and diverse nature of items that came into the Works for attention is this set of London Underground stock from the Central Line.

Looking distinctly travel weary is ex-LNER A3 4-6-2 No 4472 *Flying Scotsman* following her epic visit to Alice Springs, Australia in August 1989. The locomotive covered 4,000 miles in 27 days, travelling from Melbourne to Adelaide and Sydney.

8. CREWE DIESEL DEPOT

Crewe Diesel Depot was originally designed as an 'Examination and Repair Depot' for steam locomotives and with that in mind building work started in the summer of 1955. In spite of this British Railways was in the midst of a major modernisation programme to replace steam traction and before the Depot opened in the autumn of 1957 the facility had been assigned to maintain diesel locomotives. Twenty-five years later, as an employee of Potteries bus company, PMT Ltd, I worked with British Rail planners to implement revised bus operations during the station's closure in 1985. Through these meetings I was given official permission to visit the Depot on a Sunday to look around and take a few pictures – and I still feel very privileged that I was allowed to do this. The following pictures are set out as a snapshot in time, just as I took them. I have not attempted to list all the locos in each picture and I name an area of the depot only if it was described to me at the time, and it is written in my 5p Woolworth notebook! All but three of the photographs were taken on Sunday 7th November 1982, making an early Christmas present for me!

The main locomotive allocation at the Depot then was class 08, 25, 40 and 47, and two examples are shown here with 40096 and 47532.

The Diesel Depot stabling roads as viewed from the end of No 1 platform at the station. For most enthusiasts at the time this was as close as you were likely to get. Seen here on 1st September 1982 are classes 08, 25, 40 and 45.

From Nantwich Road there was an access road that ran down to the Diesel Depot and Training School. At the end of that road was the crossing at which you would have been stopped from proceeding further! However, on this occasion I was allowed through and got this picture of class 83 No 83012 heading towards the stabling roads. Pottering along behind is a formation of four class 85s heading in the same direction.

Another view from No 1 platform this time of the fuelling racks with 47531 and 40082 being refuelled. The 47 then ran round and passed through the washing plant.

At the north end of the Diesel Depot a number of departmental vehicles appeared from time to time and on 1st September 1982 there was 'Sandite' rail cleaning machine ADB 97750 (converted from a DMU) and Snow Plough ADB 965233.

Looking south at the Inspection Testing Bay (No1 Road) as a member of staff gets to grips with a steam lance to clean the pits. Class 25 No 25308 stands at the head of another 25 and a class 40.

Facing north, the middle roads are occupied by a class 25, just behind a set of Matterson Jacks, a class 47 positioned at the wheel lathe and class 40 No 40177 on the extreme right.

Things seem to be a little cramped at the north end of No 2 and No 3 Roads as class 40 No 40096 and 25194 stand alongside an 08 shunter and a class 25.

Facing south in the middle roads with class 25 No 25042 in the centre and 25059 to its right. Also seen is a class 47, and just to the rear of the pair of 25s is a class 40.

Raised on the Matterson Jacks at the south end of No 5 Road is class 47 No 47187 in the process of having its bogies removed for inspection whilst 25226 stands at the far right.

Class 40 No 40001 is the centre of attention in this view of bays 6, 6A and 7 (south) with the Wharton 2½-ton overhead crane seen clearly in the background.

During most weekends locomotives would be parked in the access roads at the south end of the Depot. In this view an unidentified class 47 stands on the road into 6A Bay and 25224 is on the road into Bay 6. On the right class 25 Nos 25224 plus 25242 and 08703 stand at the entrance to No 5 Road.

At the south entrance to No 2 Road, class 40 No 40195 awaits its turn to receive some attention. The reason for the Mk 2 coaches being stabled in front of the Diesel Depot was unknown.

Looking in the direction of the station are the stabling roads for diesel locos with AC electric locos stabled at the side of the main line. Class 33 No 33024 is in residence having worked up from Cardiff the previous day. The electric locos are class 83012 and the class 85s as seen on page 137. Interestingly 83012 became a 'Railtrack 89' loco No 89535 and originally preserved by Pete Waterman. It is now in preservation with the AC Locomotive Group following its purchase in 1997.

It would be only a few years after this photograph was taken that these stabling roads became full of condemned diesel and electric locomotives waiting for the scrap yard. Looking southwards the lines to the West Coast Main Line run just behind class 40 No 40128, complete with its white-painted handrails and steps.

Further down the sidings and facing the station a number of class 47s are present and on the left is class 47 No 47250 a long way from its home base at Bristol Bath Road–West Coast Main Line extreme right

Facing south again, class 40 No 40046 stands just ahead of a train of oil tanks with the Depot to its right and in the background are class 47s, 47539 and 47201. Seen in the extreme left background is the carriage shed at South Junction, now the commercial railway operation, LMWR, operated by Pete Waterman.

Moving back towards the South Junction another group of locomotives is stabled here with 40199 standing in front of three class 08 shunters and a pair of class 25s.

A closer view of class 47/5 No 47539 'Rochdale Pioneer' and class 47/2 No 47201 as they stand next to the oil tanks which are making a delivery to the three 10,000-gallon storage tanks situated at the right of the picture.

Class 40 No 40019 is seen here on the stop blocks at the far end of the stabling roads and in the foreground a through line connects with the Depot and Shrewsbury line. By this date the 40 was withdrawn from traffic and it was to be the first of many condemned locos that were to occupy these sidings in later years.

Class 47/3 No 47324 stands at rest in the Diesel Depot stabling roads and opposite Crewe South Junction signal box. The original box, with 247 levers, was opened by the LNWR in 1907 but this 'concrete bunker', for that is how it was constructed, was opened by the LMS in 1940 as the Second World War got underway.

Attached to 40199 are three of the Depot's 22 resident shunters with my friend Dave Thornton giving them a close inspection.

Having just completed checks for oil, fuel and coolant, resident class 08 No 08633 is started up prior to resuming shunting duties.

Another of the Depot's 08s No 08927 is seen here at the north end of the Diesel Depot propelling class 47 No 47066 into the yard.

9. CREWE HERITAGE CENTRE

The Crewe Heritage Centre, or 'Railway Age' as it is now known, opened to the public on 4th July 1987 as a museum to railway activities in the Crewe area. It was completed just two years after the remodelling of Crewe Station, which rendered the main signal boxes at Crewe North Junction, Crewe South Junction and the Station's 'A' box. Crewe North Junction signal box and the adjacent land on which it stood had been in railway use since the 1840s when the Grand Junction Railway built a locomotive works on the site. Unfortunately the site available for the museum was later reduced in size when it was decided to sell off part of the land to accommodate a large supermarket and car park. This chapter covers the early years and illustrates some of the comings and goings during that time.

The Heritage Centre was justly proud in July 1988 when the oldest working original steam engine *'Lion'* paid a short visit during the locomotive's 150th Anniversary year. The 0-4-2 was built for the Liverpool & Manchester Railway in 1838 by Todd Kitson & Laird and when it was withdrawn in 1859 it went to the Mersey Docks and Harbour Board to work as a static steam boiler. It remained there anonymously for many years until, in the 1920s, the LMS discovered its whereabouts and purchased the locomotive, restoring it to working condition and in 1953 it was loaned by British Railways to star in the film *'The Titfield Thunderbolt'*. It now resides at the Liverpool Museum.

Two days after the official opening on 6th July 1987 ex-LMS 8f 2-8-0 No 48151 is in light steam while ex-BR 4-6-2 No 71000 *'Duke of Gloucester'* provides super-power for brake van rides.

Because the Heritage Centre was to provide servicing facilities for visiting steam locomotives and machines that were going to work passenger services to the North Wales coast an original water column and fire devil were installed. Alongside is a visitor from Carnforth, ex-LMS Ivatt 2-6-0 No 6441.

One of the main attractions on the Heritage site is the North Junction Signal Box and it is seen here on 7th July 1987 complete with an 'Eagle' from Crewe Works' Eagle Bridge. For a few months after opening there was also a Collectors Corner selling various items of old railway equipment and signage.

Part of North Junction's impressive bank of 214 miniature levers that controlled signals, points and crossings before that function was transferred to the new Signalling Control Centre on 12th June 1985. This signal box was opened on 25th August 1940 and replaced the former 1906-built cabin that was equipped with a 266 lever LNWR frame.

Variety at the Heritage Centre on 8th July 1988 as Tysley's 0-6-0PT No 7752 shunts exhibits No's 47001 and 25083 while the centre's new arrival, the APT set, stands on track which was originally laid as the APT's permanent location.

A general view of the Heritage site on 7th July 1987, from the North Junction Signal Box steps. The museum's main exhibition hall is seen in the background with several exhibits standing in the sidings. On the extreme left is the Chester line and the rail connection to the Heritage Centre. The sloping brick structure leading up to the box is what remains of the 1906 signal box and 'Spider Bridge' that carried a narrow gauge railway from the old works to the station-passing right through the middle of that signal box!

In the main exhibition hall on 6th November 1988 is the Heritage Centre's class 47, No 47192, out of the weather and about to undergo a significant restoration job over the following year or so. This particular area had permanent track laid to the floor and is currently occupied by Pete Waterman's LNWR machine shops that forms part of a working feature for visitors.

On 9th July 1988 a view of the site looking towards the town with the all-black livery class 08 shunter No 08907 and Crewe station 'A' box and the APT set 370003 being made ready for opening to visitors.

When this picture was taken on 2nd January 1989 almost all of the class 40s, with the exception of those re-tained for preservation, had been cut up or as in this case the cab end had been removed for private sale. Here is one end of 40088 and presumably destined for someone's back garden-and no doubt minus the graffiti, "Sulzer Rules"

With 71000 *'Duke of Gloucester'* out working a steam special, the day's brake van rides on 7th July 1987 were in the charge of ex-LMS 8f No 48151 seen here passing Station 'A' signal box for a trip along the short demon-stration track. It carries the *Crewe Heritage Centre* headboard that would be displayed by a number of visiting locomotives whilst working steam excursions from Crewe to the North Wales Coast and elsewhere.

Although class 47s No 47001 and 47192 had been allocated to the Heritage Centre to represent the type, another of the class, 47015, made a brief visit on 18th June 1988 and through the generosity of Crewe Works to donate various essential components.

When this picture was taken on 24th June 1990 things were changing at the Heritage Centre. Part of the land had been sold to developers and in this view, looking towards the museum building, the frames of a new superstore building were going up where once stood the APT and other extended sidings. This action curtailed any significant expansion of the museum site. However, in later years Pete Waterman set up his LNWR Company to restore steam locomotives and Exeter Signal Box was rebuilt here by preservationists which today provides an important working feature.

On 2nd January 1989 two new arrivals at the Heritage Centre were 'Austerity' 0-6-0 saddle tanks from Chatterley Whitfield Mining Museum, *'Joseph'* (Hunslet works No 3163) built in 1944 and *'Robert'* (Hudswell Clarke works No 1752) built in 1943. The locomotives, both originally from Bold Colliery, had been transferred to Crewe for restoration, after which one was to return to Chatterley Whitfield whilst the other was to remain at the Heritage Centre on static display.

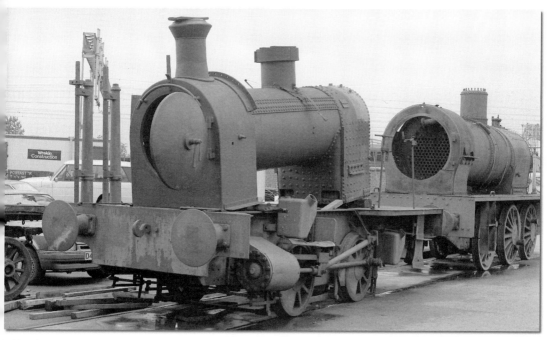

This photograph, taken 18 months later, on 24th June 1990 shows *'Joseph'*, (right) in an early stage of its restoration and on the left Kerr Stuart 0-4-0ST, No 4388, which had been transferred to the Heritage Centre from Foxfield Railway Society for restoration. The locomotive was purchased from Brookfield Foundry (former Kerr Stuart Works) Stoke-on-Trent by Foxfield in 1983. Both locomotives were subsequently returned to steam.

On 9th July 1988 a number of visiting locomotives were on site, one of which was ex-Great Western Railway 5600 class 0-6-2T No 5619. The class was a Collet design introduced in 1924 and 193 of the type were built to haul freight traffic through the Welsh valleys.

On the same day is this Robert Stevens & Hawthorn 0-6-0T locomotive No 7597 (actually its works number) built in 1949 in relatively small numbers and mainly for power station work. The locomotive currently resides at Peak Rail's Darley Dale site.

On 1st July 1990 the brake van rides were being hauled by another visiting locomotive, *'Jane Derbyshire'*, a 0-4-0ST built in 1929 by Andrew Barclay & Sons Kilmarnock, works number 1969. When built for the Carlisle Plaster & Cement Co its original name was J.N. Derbyshire but whilst in private ownership at Carnforth it was renamed Jane Derbyshire. The locomotive is now at the Ribble Steam Railway Preston as a static exhibit.

On 1st July 1990, after returning from its tour of Australia the previous year, ex LNER A3 4-6-2 No 4472 *'Flying Scotsman'* receives a bit of attention before the locomotive's return to steam in the UK and its appearance at the Crewe Works Open Day on the 21st July that year. To commemorate its record-breaking non-stop run in Australia a special plaque was attached to the nameplate; "*On August 8th 1989 this locomotive achieved the World's longest non-stop run for steam traction 422 miles 7.59 chains between Parkes and Broken Hill in New South Wales Australia*"

Dr Beet, a railway enthusiast who was one of the founders of what is now known as Steamtown Carnforth, acquired a number of locomotives including this Andre Chapelon class 231 Pacific No 231K22 *'La France'* seen here on 14th April 1990.

On the same day another of Dr Beet's acquisitions this time an impressive Deutsche Reichsbahn-Gesellschaft (DRG) class 01 Pacific No 011104. Both locomotives left the Heritage Centre as quickly as they came and are now believed to be back on the continent.

As work progressed on building the supermarket the APT was displaced from its original site and because of the length involved it could only be re-instated at the side of the West Coast Main Line, maybe a more appropriate place. On 14th April 1990 some heavy lifting gear was required to accomplish this task, as can be seen working in the background.

On 24th February 1991 the Safeway supermarket was finished and as a tribute to the railway land on which the store was built the company acquired this 0-4-0 saddle tank loco 'Elizabeth' and mounted it outside the entrance. It was built by Avonside Engine Co Bristol in 1922 for the Sydenham Gas Works. In 1955 it was converted to oil burning but returned to coal firing before being purchased by Sir William McAlpine in 1969. It transferred to Carnforth in 1986 under new ownership and remained there until 1991 when it was purchased by Safeway plc.

INDEX